King of the Rocks

Written by Samantha Montgomerie
Illustrated by Sanjay Charlton

Collins

Zip can chop.

Zip can kick.

Zip is fit.

He jogs up.

Zip is quick.

7

Zip chops.

Bang!

Zip tips the rats.

Zip kicks.

A box is on the rats.

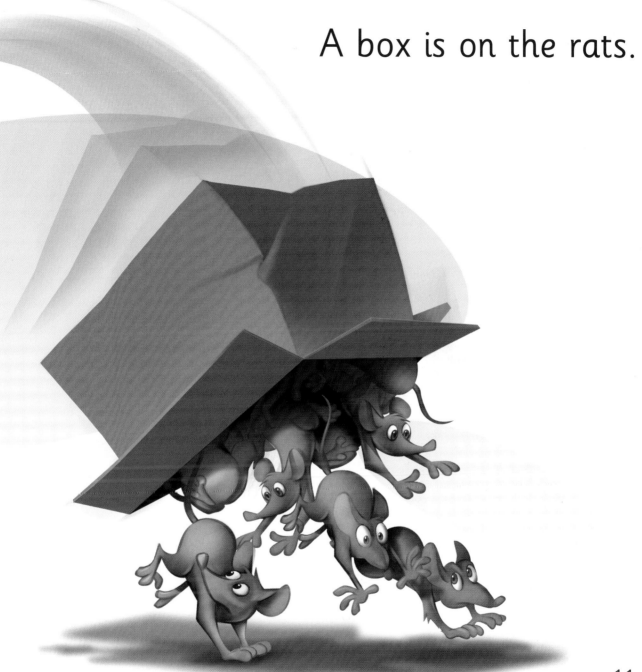

Zip is the King of Kicks!

/ch/

14

After reading

Letters and Sounds: Phase 3

Word count: 40

Focus phonemes: /j/ /x/ /z/ /qu/ /ch/ /th/ /ng/ /nk/

Common exception words: he, the, of

Curriculum links: Physical development; Understanding the world

Early learning goals: Reading: read and understand simple sentences; use phonic knowledge to decode regular words and read them aloud accurately; read some common irregular words

Developing fluency

- Your child may enjoy hearing you read the book.
- Take turns to read a page, encouraging your child to reread a sentence if they have difficulties with, for example, the exception words such as **he**. On page 6, read the speech bubble together. On page 8 encourage your child to read **Bang!** dramatically.

Phonic practice

- Focus on the letter sounds /ch/, /qu/ and /th/.
- Ask your child to sound out and blend the following:

  ch/o/p/s   qu/i/ck   th/a/nk/s

- Challenge your child to point to the letters that make the /ch/, /qu/ and /th/ sound in each word.
- Look at the "I spy sounds" pages (14 and 15) together. Take turns to find a word in the picture containing a /ch/ or /th/ sound. (e.g. *chop, cheeks, cherries, chocolate cake, chairs, checks*; *thorns, three, cloth, thimble*)

Extending vocabulary

- On page 2, ask your child what **chop** means. (e.g. *cuts, splits*) Can your child think of other things people might chop? (e.g. *wood, carrots, onions*)
- On page 7, focus on the cat's name, **Zip**. Talk about other meanings of "zip". (*to move fast, a clothes fastening*) Does your child think **Zip** is a good name for this cat?